Dexter's Business Builders

DEXTER YAGER

Published by InterNET Services Corporation

Library of Congress Cataloging-in-Publication Data

Yager, Dexter.
[Business builders]
Dexter's business builders / Dexter Yager.
p. cm.
ISBN 0-8423-1630-2 (pbk)
1. Business—Quotations, maxims, etc. I. Title.

PN6084.B87Y35 1995
650—dc20 95-4709

Printed in the United States of America

01 00 99 98 97 96 95
7 6 5 4 3 2 1

I love each of you

regardless of what you do.

Respect you must earn

through your performance.

Dexter Hager

The illustrations in this book are symbolic of freedom, goals, dreams, and new horizons that inspire Dexter Yager as he continues to build his business and help others achieve their dreams.

Contents

Dream the Possible Dream

A person with big dreams is more powerful than a person with all the facts.

Dreams are the touchstones of our character.

Live on the dream of tomorrow—that
is how you get through today.

The ache of unfulfilled dreams
is the greatest pain of all.

N
E
S

Most people in America have a dream for retirement, but retirement isn't usually a vehicle for achievement.

If the dream is big enough, the facts don't count.

A dream is something you visualize as possible; a fantasy is something you know will not come true.

Dreams are a defense mechanism against complacency.

Whoever said "Dream the impossible dream" never met one of us. We dream the "possible dream" every time we draw a circle.

The dream is the motivation.

People and rubber bands have one thing in common: They must be stretched to be effective.

Don't relive your past. Those who do, do it because they don't have a present or a future.

Every relationship in your life is a current moving you toward your dreams or away from them.

Those who earned the pin of yesterday do not control the dreams of tomorrow.

If you're going to dream big, then you're going to have to work hard to make your dreams come true.

When you change your focus, you will change your results.

Release Positive Energy with Positive Thinking

Release Positive Energy with Positive Thinking

You will maximize your potential when you are willing to give up at any moment all that you are and all that you receive to become all that you can be.

Don't live what you did; live what you are doing.

Release Positive Energy with Positive Thinking

Seed-faith is sowing what you have been given to create what you have been promised.

We see things not as they are but as they can and will be.

Release Positive Energy with Positive Thinking

Don't let the things that matter most be at the mercy of the things that matter least.

Hang-ups will hang you up.

Release Positive Energy with Positive Thinking

Champions are willing to do the things they dislike to create something they do like.

Take the negative and turn it into positive energy.

The greatest ignorance is to reject something you know nothing about.

What you see, touch, and experience determines what you desire.

What happens to you is not nearly as important as how you handle it.

End each day a little happier than when you started.

People often live their problems rather than their possibilities.

Being broke is a temporary condition; poverty is a state of mind.

Failure is a temporary experience on the way to success. It is part of the learning process.

All material things are temporary to those who believe they'll continue to achieve.

My great concern is not whether you have failed but whether you are content with your failure.

Failure is an opportunity to begin again with insight.

There is no such thing as an empty glass; it is either filled with liquid or with air. There is also no such thing as an empty mind; it is either filled with positive or negative thoughts.

Nothing is ever as bad as it first appears.

Circumstances don't change us. The way we handle circumstances changes us.

Enthusiasm is contagious. Become infectious with it.

Greatness is not the pursuit of perfection but the pursuit of completion.

I work until I'm exhausted and play until I'm bored.

The person with experience is never at the mercy of a person with a theory.

Your security is in your ability to perform.

Strive to fill your mind with good, positive, and spiritual things. If you keep your mind filled with positive thoughts, there will be no room for negative thoughts.

Control your thoughts and you control your life.

Be Wise as an Owl

Whatever you do, do it with all your might. Work at it early and late, in season and out of season, not leaving a stone unturned, and never putting off for a single hour that which can be done just as well now.

The intolerance of your present creates your future.

Some people focus on what they are going through;
champions focus on what they are going to.

You will never leave where you are until
you decide where you would rather be.

You have to close the door on your past
before you can have a future.

Don't look at where you have been;
start looking at where you can be.

A limit on what you will do puts
a limit on what you can do.

What you are willing to walk away from
determines what God will bring toward you.

N
E
S

The problem that infuriates you the most
is the problem that God has assigned you to solve.

What you hate may just reveal what
you were created to correct.

When you want something you never had, you have to do something you have never done.

There is no luck involved in success. Luck is a way of saying you don't have what it takes.

Take a tragedy and make a cause out of it.
A cause will unite people.

Establish the cause. It creates the energy.

There are two quick paths to failure: take nobody's counsel and take everybody's counsel.

Knowing when to keep quiet and when to speak up is wisdom.

You will be the same in five years as you are today except for three things: the people with whom you associate, the books you read, and the type of information you hear.

Kindness is more important than perfection.

You can either be flexible or dogmatic.
Bend more and bark less.

No matter how thin you slice it,
there are always two sides.

Attitude! It can shoot you straight to the stars or dump you into the depths of despair.

A smile and a handshake can break down even the toughest barriers.

Building Blocks
for
Your Business

We each need a lifestyle that doesn't end
when our earning power does.

There is no security on this earth—only opportunity.

N
E
S

It's not how many people you sponsor—it's how many people you help others sponsor.

Measure your progress by how many circles you draw.

Draw circles until you find the person, then develop the person by counseling and building a good relationship.

We either triple people or we cripple people.

The atmosphere you permit
determines the result you produce.

Groups grow according to our expectations.
Keep them high.

How do you contact strangers?
You don't. You make them friends first.

If you try to rope in every contact you see,
you may find yourself tied up in knots.

Building Blocks for Your Business

Work and build where you are celebrated instead of where you are tolerated.

When you leave a group, be missed.

Building Blocks for Your Business

If you have a long-distance group but that group doesn't have one, you haven't duplicated yourself. Your security in this business is having a long-distance group backed up by a long-distance group backed up by a long-distance group.

One of the best principles of this business is that no one can really try to help themselves without helping another.

When you take your eyes off yourself and put them on others, your business will grow.

Building Blocks for Your Business

When you give a presentation, keep your mind on what you can convey rather than on what you can get out of it.

Give people a second chance—run them through the system again.

Building Blocks for Your Business

Your pin level will only be as big as the number of problems you solve.

The people who solve problems make the biggest bucks.

Building Blocks for Your Business

If you treat the business like a job,
you will always have a job income.

You will never be promoted until you become
overqualified for your present assignment.

Ignore the weaknesses in others and focus only on their strengths.

Build on strengths in people—your own and others.

Somewhere along the line, you've got to realize that Diamond is simply a decision, and the results will follow the work.

Don't imitate—duplicate.

Those who do not respect your time
will not respect your wisdom either.

Those who do not respect your business
disqualify themselves for a relationship.

More people quit this business because their feelings are hurt than because they're not making enough money.

Don't step on people's toes; they will walk out limping.

Building Blocks for Your Business

We need to uplift each other, find each other's strengths, respect each other's lines of sponsorship, and love each other more.

Advice is best taken in small doses.

Lead by Example

The size of a leader is determined by the depth of the conviction, the height of the ambition, the breadth of the vision, and the reach of the love.

The most effective leadership is by example.

A leader is one who knows the way,
goes the way, and shows the way.

Eagles don't flock—you have
to find them one at a time.

A good leader takes a little more than his or her share of the blame and a little less than his or her share of the credit.

Leaders walk the talk.

Lead by Example

It is wonderful when the people believe in their leader, but it is more wonderful when the leader believes in the people.

You manage things; you lead people.

Lead by Example

The key to successful leadership today
is influence, not authority.

People will stay with you
because you believe in them.

A big person is one who makes us feel bigger
and better when we are with them.

It's nice to be important,
but it's more important to be nice.

Lead by Example

One of the greatest gifts leaders can give others is hope.

Never underestimate the power of hope—worlds have been built on it.

Lead by Example

In order to make a fire burn, you fan the live coals. In order to keep your organization strong and fired up, it is imperative that you find and motivate the leaders or potential leaders in your organization. This means working anywhere that leadership is evident, regardless of how far down the line it might be.

Lead by Example

A wise leader inspires and motivates rather than intimidates and manipulates.

People do not follow programs; they follow leaders who inspire them.

Lead by Example

Ask yourself every day: Am I building my dream by growing and building up people or building my dream and then using people to do it?

Always look back . . . someone may need a helping hand.

Love and respect are not automatically given to someone in a leadership position. They must be earned.

Either you control your attitude or your attitude controls you.

Leadership is getting people to help you when they're not obligated to do so.

Lead, follow, or get out of the way.

Lead by Example

Nothing so conclusively proves people's ability to lead others as what they do from day to day to lead themselves.

We teach what we know; we reproduce what we are.

An individual must be big enough to admit mistakes, smart enough to profit from them, and strong enough to correct them.

People are changed by example.

You cannot lead anyone else farther than you have been able to go yourself.

Things don't just happen; someone makes them happen.

Lead by Example

When you bring up kids, you have to teach things over and over and over again. As a leader, you must counsel again and again and again. The biggest part of this business is the relationship, not the money. Teach that over and over and over.

Lead by Example

Six people you know will get into this business and become Diamonds with or without you! Which way do you prefer?

A leader who develops people *adds;* a leader who develops leaders *multiplies!*

Lead by Example

When you get right down to it, one of the most important tasks of a leader is to eliminate his people's excuses for failure.

It's not the size of the person in the fight; it's the size of the fight in the person.

Lead by Example

I study the lives of great men and women, and I find that those who get to the top are the ones who do the jobs they have in hand with everything they have inside of them and with all the energy and enthusiasm they can muster.

The proof of faith is effort.

Lead by Example

Leadership is a privilege, and with privilege comes responsibility.

Never discuss a problem with someone incapable of solving it.

Leaders who win the respect of others deliver more than they promise, not promise more than they can deliver.

Good leaders must first become good servants.

Lead by Example

Favor begins to happen the moment you solve a problem for someone.

One of the tests of leadership is the ability to recognize a problem before it becomes an emergency.

Lead by Example

A wise leader resolves conflicts peaceably, not forcibly.

A good leader is a person who can step on your toes without messing up your shine.

Lead by Example

Real leaders are ordinary people with extraordinary determination.

Even eagles need a push sometimes.

Lead by Example

It's not disloyal to go around a person to build depth, but always maintain the relationship. You don't have to lose the relationship while following the leg to find other leaders.

Leadership is developed, not discovered.

Lead by Example

In order for your kids and family to come first, the distributors must come first.

Anything you gain is based on how you love and serve people.

Lead by Example

Lord, when I am wrong, make me willing to change; when I am right, make me easy to live with. So strengthen me, in that the power of my example will far exceed the authority of my rank.

Your attitude will make you or break you.

Proverbs to Ponder

What you are driving is not important.
What is important is what's driving you.

Show me a thoroughly satisfied individual,
and I will show you a failure.

People decide their habits . . . their habits decide their future.

Those who won't be counseled can't be helped.

You either multiply your problems or you multiply your luxuries.

Don't confuse mere inconveniences with real problems.

The quality of your preparation determines the quality of your performance.

The worst thing you can do is lower the requirements.

Proverbs to Ponder

If you can't love your neighbors, then like them a little.

Your rewards in life are determined by the problems you solve for others.

Proverbs to Ponder

We make a living by what we get,
but we make a life by what we give.

Nothing is remembered so well as good manners.

Aim for the Stars

Aim for the Stars

To effectively manage your time, I recommend
you take care of the minutes;
the hours will take care of themselves.

Set your goals and believe they will come true. And
with hard work and the right attitude, they will!

Aim for the Stars.

If you are not hurting, you are not going to grow. You only hurt when you know you are capable of having something you don't yet have.

Realistically assess your own abilities and inspire others to help you achieve your goals and dreams.

The only way our kids can have a better life than we have is to teach them more and work them harder.

Concentrate on lifting people up,
not putting people down.

There are no losers out there. There are people who have temporarily lost their way. Help them back onto the right track and you'll be a real winner.

Spend your time and energy creating and developing, not criticizing.

You cannot achieve anything worthwhile for yourself or for others without first developing a heartfelt belief in your ability to accomplish the task.

Nothing of value comes without effort.

Whatever you try to do in life, try with all your heart to do it well. Whatever you devote yourself to, devote yourself to it completely. When pursuing goals, great and small, always do so thoroughly and diligently.

Don't major on the minors; major on the majors.

Things only help us to reach people. Things do not bring happiness unless we share them with people.

Nothing can replace the truth when doing business. Deception has no place in business or in life.

Aim for the Stars

Amway is a business vehicle which makes nearly everything else old-fashioned.

Amway at its worst is better than anything else at its best.

N
E
S

Whether it is losing weight or increasing your net worth—whatever your goal or dream—you *can* achieve it!

Be a winner, not a whiner.

Success Is What You Make It

Success is a part of all of us.
We just have to dig down and find that successful part of us and help it grow.

Don't equate material wealth with real success.

Ninety-five percent of achieving anything is knowing what you want and paying the price to get it.

Pay now, play later; play now, pay later.

Success Is What You Make It

Remember: The closer you get to success, the harder it is to reach it.

I'll help you pass me, but you'll have your tongue hanging out when you do.

Never be too proud to admit your failure
nor too humble to admit your success.

The only place success comes
before work is in the dictionary.

I have not built this business on material wealth; I have built it on relationships. The wealth is a result of the relationships.

A person excels inside when they excel outside.

In reading the lives of great individuals, I found that the first victory they won was over themselves; with all of them, self-discipline came first.

Success results more from hard work than talent.

A person who is successful has simply formed the habit of doing things that unsuccessful people will not do.

The secret of your future is hidden in your daily routine.

Most people who succeed in the face of seemingly impossible conditions are people who simply won't allow themselves to quit.

You can't build a business on what you're going to do.

I despise the people who criticize and minimize the enterprise of the others whose enterprise has made them rise above the people who criticize.

If you don't stand for something, you'll fall for anything.

Success is created by making
the inconvenient convenient.

Ability may get you to the top,
but it takes character to keep you there.